Good Thai Girl: Bangkok Guide to Nice Thai Girls... Not Hookers

Linda Chomatree

Published by Linda Chomatree, 2025.

While every precaution has been taken in the preparation of this book, the publisher assumes no responsibility for errors or omissions, or for damages resulting from the use of the information contained herein.

GOOD THAI GIRL: BANGKOK GUIDE TO NICE THAI GIRLS... NOT HOOKERS

First edition. October 4, 2025.

Copyright © 2025 Linda Chomatree.

ISBN: 979-8215532652

Written by Linda Chomatree.

Table of Contents

You Will Never Understand Thailand (Without This Book)

Maybe you've dreamed of having a Thai girlfriend or wife. Maybe you'll be traveling to or living in Bangkok and have heard about the greatness (or the evils) of Thai women. Or maybe you've already met a Thai woman and want to know what the hell is going on.

If you're planning to operate on the rules from your home country—presumably the US, but this warning is just as valid if you plan on using the rules from any country that's not Thailand, even an Asian country that's not Thailand—you're going to fall on your butt.

You might be totally unable to meet the kinds of girls you're after. Or you may meet girls who aren't who you think they are. Or you may meet girls who end up mistreating you, emotionally or financially or otherwise, once you've committed to them, emotionally or financially or otherwise. Anyway, it won't be good.

This is something Thai people always say, and I really hope you can believe me: Thailand is very different from every other country. I really don't believe many of the standard things that Thai people tell foreigners (for example, "foreigners can never understand Thailand"—I don't believe that at all), but having visited many foreign countries, lived in the UK and US, and met and worked with people from all over the world, I can really assuredly tell you that Thailand is more unusual, "more unique" (yeah, I know, that's supposed to be grammatically wrong), more unlike any other country you've been to.

Many Thai people believe, even if they won't tell you, that being unusual makes Thailand the best. Best culture, oldest culture, good culture, unique culture, every other country is full of savages—I don't believe any of that, but many Thai people do believe it, and they'll use it as justification for why you can never understand Thailand or you can never fit in Thailand or even why you can never get a Thai girlfriend or wife who's not a prostitute. I don't believe that at all. But I do believe that if you parachute into Bangkok without studying and considering how it's different from your home country, you will indeed never understand Thailand.

Thai girls, Thai women are, of course, a multitude. One of the funniest things I've heard foreign visitors to Thailand say is that all Thai women are basically the same—look the same, talk the same, act the same. That to me indicates that the foreigner has only been meeting one very specific sort of Thai woman. Now, if the foreigner is a visiting medical researcher, maybe all the Thai women he's been meeting have been medical researchers, and that's the only type of Thai woman he knows. But the more common situation is that a foreign visitor to Thailand has been meeting only one type of Thai woman: prostitutes. And more specifically, prostitutes working in foreigner-oriented bars.

Before writing this book, I researched what was already out there, in books and online, about dating contemporary Thai women. I found that just about all the foreign experts characterize all Thai women as sexually open, passionately hot-tempered, economical with the truth, proficient in spoken but not written English, and always in financial crisis. Oh, and Thai women's appearance as always described by foreigners: dark-skinned, short in stature, revealingly dressed.

Okay, so imagine that you're an American, and your Thai friend just moved to America, and he tells you he knows what American women are like. According to your Thai friend, all American women: have large breast implants, have many tattoos, go by names like "Porsche" and "Delicious," often abuse drugs and alcohol, work at night, and are really great at pole-dancing. Your Thai friend, imagine, might even write a book titled *Guide to American Women* based on this information, and post his recommendations on the Thai-language internet, saying that, for example, the most important thing about finding an American girlfriend is finding one who offers two-for-one lap dances.

You're laughing. But that's how the "guides to Thai women" sound to a Thai person. There's (maybe) nothing wrong with coming to Thailand and spending all your time with bar prostitutes. Just as there's (maybe) nothing wrong with coming to America and spending all your time with strippers. But in either case, you should realize that you're meeting only a very small and very unusual subset of the female population.

I'm a Thai woman. I'm not a hooker. Actually, many Thai women aren't hookers. But many are. Whatever. It's their life, and I don't claim to be any better than they are, but it does annoy me when foreigners assume I'm a hooker just because I'm Thai.

When I was a university student in Bangkok, two of my female friends and I decided to go on a trip to Singapore for the weekend. It was my first trip abroad without my parents. Our very first encounter with Singaporean perceptions of Thai women—the taxi driver from the airport to the hotel pretty much openly assumed we were prostitutes and was advising us that we can make much better money in Singapore than in Thailand.

Can you imagine being thought to be a prostitute just because you answer that you're from a certain country?

Also kind of funny, but not harmful, is when I tell people (outside Thailand) that I'm Thai, and they think I'm lying. Most Thai women that foreigners encounter, bar prostitutes, have a very specific ethnic look and a specific way of acting and dressing. People of the Issan-Lao ethnicity make up 30% of the Thai population, but they make up almost 100% of foreigner-oriented prostitutes. And the look of foreigner-oriented prostitutes is the "Thai person look" that people get used to, and then they can't believe it when someone like me, who is not from that ethnic background, calls themselves Thai.

Of course that's not purely a Thai phenomenon. When I studied in the US, I had a classmate named Eduardo Chen. As you might be able to tell from his last name, Eduardo's ancestors, about a hundred fifty years ago, emigrated to Mexico from China. His family has lived in Mexico for many generations now (and they have managed to intermarry only with other people of Chinese Mexican origin), and he considers himself fully Mexican.

But can you imagine when Americans would ask him "Where are you from?" and he'd say "I'm Mexican," and they'd think he's joking.

"No man, really, where are you from?"

"I'm Mexican."

"No, come on man, stop playing around, where are you from?"

"I'm Mexican."

And so on. Just because Eduardo isn't dark-skinned, doesn't wear a sombrero, and doesn't play in a mariachi band. He doesn't care, but you can imagine it gets tiring, and he either ignores it, or pulls out his Mexican driver's license if convincing the person really matters to him.

And I get the same thing when I tell people I'm Thai. Either "No, Linda, ha ha, really, where are you from?" (Since "I'm Thai" is taken as a sex joke I guess) or "Oh, we say *Taiwanese* not *Thai* for people from Taiwan." (Hey, good guess, but I really am Thai, from Thailand.)

So, guess what. Not every Mexican plays in a mariachi band or mows suburban lawns in Texas, even though those are the Mexicans you might see in the media and maybe in your town. And not every Thai woman is a prostitute, and not every Thai woman looks like someone from the Issan ethnic group, even though those are the Thai women you might see in the media and even in your town.

The reason I'm telling you these things is for your benefit, not mine. I'm not likely to meet you in person, and even if I did, I wouldn't care that much what you thought of me. But if you're trying to meet other Thai women, for dating or whatever other purposes, it's good, really good, to know the subject matter.

If I'm not a bargirl, then who am I?

I guess you can say I'm from Bangkok's non-bargirl female masses.

I'm not a professional writer. I have an undergraduate degree in business from a Thai university, and then an MA from a US university. I work in a family business that's involved in commercial real estate in the US, so I get to often travel between the US and Thailand and compare cultures, and also compare Thais' and Americans' perceptions of each other.

You could say I'm from an above-average socioeconomic background for Thailand, although if you compare my family's income and wealth to US standards, it's really nothing special. And you could say that insofar as I'm not a professional writer, this book is a bit of a vanity project for me. It's fun to write, and I hope to inform people and get the word out. And maybe even the next time some non-Thai person asks me "hey, how can I meet a nice Thai girl... but not a ladyboy or a hooker!" I can send him to this book, rather than having to tell him that giving him a full answer would require writing a book, not a five-minute advice session or text message.

What I hope this book gives you:

1. An understanding of Thai women that goes beyond bar prostitutes (with a brief discussion of prostitutes too). Knowing how to identify types of Thai women—and yes, Thailand is a pretty structured society, and Thai women really do tend to fall into certain set types, and yes, that will include discussion of ladyboys (Why do foreigners always worry about ladyboys? Outside the tourist prostitution areas, ladyboys are a rarity in Thailand.)
2. Understanding of Thai culture as it applies to dating, especially as it applies to dating non-prostitutes.
3. Specific ways to identify, meet, and attract Thai women who fit your dating criteria—both online and offline, but with the assumption that you will travel to Bangkok or are already here.
4. Managing your relationship with a Thai woman.

I'm sorry that I can't promise you that you'll be swimming in hot Thai pussy within 24 hours of reading this book, nor that you'll have a date with a supermodel upon landing in Bangkok. If I promised anything like that, you'd know I was a scammer, right? (Just like those "You can get rich buying these gems and reselling them in America" street scammers in Bangkok... watch out for those guys by the way!)

I will give you really, really good advice. To the best of my abilities, which are considerable. I don't think many Thai women are able or willing to provide this guidance, at least not to strangers or a public audience.

So consider yourself lucky. And after you read this book, consider yourself educated about good Thai girls.

Social Ruin of Dating a Prostitute

I'm writing about *how* to avoid dating hookers in Thailand. I think I should also discuss *why* you should, or might want to, avoid dating hookers in Thailand.

The funny and ironic thing is that most Western men already know very well why they wouldn't date a prostitute back in their home country. Then they come to Thailand and date or marry a prostitute, and somehow expect it to be totally different from dating or marrying a prostitute in their country—maybe because the prostitute he met here in Thailand was so cute-looking, or because she told him she loves him, or because he thinks Thai prostitutes are typical or average Thai women. We all tend to have some cultural blinders when encountering a new place: we tend to forget that a lot of the laws of physics and mathematics and human interaction are the same no matter where in the world you are.

So let's talk about some of those reasons specifically. Actually, most of these reasons apply equally well in first-world Western countries, but somehow most guys pretend that it's not the case.

1. Surprise surprise: prostitutes are desperate for money, and are ready to make you feel good, physically and emotionally, for money. Money is their prime concern. They became prostitutes because they are desperate for money. No shit, right? That's the very definition of a prostitute. You would know this right off the bat back home in your country. So how is it that lots of foreign guys come to Thailand, and then are shocked or disappointed or angry that the prostitutes they meet are really desperate for money, and focus their lives on money? Maybe they somehow believe that in Thailand, prostitutes aren't prostitutes. Guess what: even in Thailand, a prostitute is a prostitute. No, I don't look down on prostitutes. But I think it's important to be honest to recognize that prostitution is

about making someone (usually a man) feel good, in exchange for money—and when a woman dedicates her working life to prostitution, and when you meet her when she's doing exactly that job, it's going to have a huge effect on your relationship.

2. If you date or marry a prostitute, your credibility with Thai people is going to be approximately -9,000. For almost all Thai people, even the poor, prostitutes are acceptable to provide sexual services for an hour, but most definitely not acceptable to date or marry. If you date or marry a prostitute, Thai people will look down on you at every chance they get. They may let you know it, or not. One very common scenario: a Thai person invites their foreign male friend to a social event (say, a group dinner or a family outing). The foreign male friend brings their prostitute girlfriend or wife to the social event. Everything seems to go well—but the foreign male is never invited to any more social outings with that Thai person or that Thai person's social circle. When he asks his Thai friend why they haven't had any meetups recently? Oh, everybody's been busy, and the weather's been so hot, and so on and so on. The real reason: Thai people consider prostitutes to be a lower species of life, something like an untouchable caste, and they absolutely don't want to socialize with them, even if that prostitute is their friend's wife or girlfriend. Please don't fly into a rage at me. I'm not endorsing their viewpoints. I'm only the messenger. I can't change Thai culture. I've had more experience outside of Thailand to consider these things, so I don't subscribe to these beliefs myself. But almost every Thai person subscribes to these beliefs.

3. Sexually transmitted diseases are a very real threat. Again, this is true of prostitutes anywhere in the world. I think in Thailand it's even more true because Thai prostitutes, as opposed to prostitutes in first-world countries, tend to be "flexible" about

condom use. The latest study that I read said that among formal prostitutes studied in Thailand ("formal" meaning working in a venue where you pay cash for a sex act) about 8-10% were HIV positive. But here's the kicker: study after study has found that informal prostitutes (women who have sex with foreigners for money or other benefits, often meeting them online or by working in tourist venues) have HIV infection rates of around 20-30%. And that's only HIV, the rarest STD. The rates of other diseases, such as genital herpes, are in the above-50% range. You'd know that prostitutes back in your country are likely to have STDs. Somehow many foreigners forget that the same thing is true in Thailand.

4. A woman accustomed to treating men as customers is unlikely to have loyalty to you if a better deal comes along. For a woman who's not a prostitute, there's a big emotional toll to changing from one lover to another. For a prostitute, that emotional toll has been worn away—she's been desensitized—she will walk away from you the minute she's offered a bigger spending allowance or a flashier house.

5. She will never be able to fit in anywhere outside the lowest rungs of Thai society. If you have an idea of rescuing a prostitute and sending her to school and turning her into a Thai schoolteacher or accountant or secretary—it won't happen. Thailand has an extremely rigid social structure. Thai people will make a former prostitute feel extremely unwelcome in any setting other than the prostitution business. Yes, an ex-prostitute will be able to fit in in America—if you overcome some other challenges—but never, ever in Thailand. Again: please don't be angry at me. I didn't invent Thai culture. I don't always agree with Thai culture. I'm only telling you the truth about it. What are the challenges of her fitting in in a university or office in America? See point 6, below.

6. Her educational level will be shockingly low and her worldview will be shockingly simple. There are a few simultaneous things at work here. First off: outside of a few small exceptions (the top Thai medical schools are one notable exception), pretty much all education in Thailand is atrociously bad. I mean, really bad. Or not so bad if you believe that the role of education is to create someone who is loyal to their parents and their King. But really, really bad if you think the role of education is learning to read, write, analyze, and think. Those skills almost don't exist in Thai education, except perhaps some elite $30,000/year private schools in Bangkok. So you are starting with that disadvantage with any Thai person, other than the elite levels who have studied at elite private schools and foreign universities. But there's more when you're dealing with a prostitute. A prostitute is a prostitute because of two particular additional disadvantages: she is from a poor rural place in Thailand, and her educational level, even within the Thai system is very low. I know that in America, even poor people finish high school, and rural high schools aren't very different in coursework from urban high schools. I know. That is absolutely not the case in Thailand. A Thai prostitute likely finished something like middle school. Thai middle school. Rural Thai middle school. Example questions I can guarantee a Thai prostitute can not answer (or if she can, it's not from learning in school): "What countries border Thailand?" "What is Thailand's form of government?" "How many weeks are in one year?" "Where is England on a map?" "What language is most commonly spoken in South America?" "What causes high tides?" "What's bigger: the moon or the sun?" "What does the Christian cross mean?" And so on. It is going to be very, very difficult for a person with this level of non-education to integrate herself into an American office or university. Not impossible but difficult.

And—depending on your tastes in conversation—it may be difficult for someone with this level of non-education for you to have a deep relationship with her.

7. The last one is related to many of the other ones. Prostitution is not an easy life. It's not The Happy Hooker. Prostitutes carry a lot of emotional scars—sometimes physical ones too. It's like post-traumatic stress disorder. And it can surface in the strangest ways, often manifesting to the husband or boyfriend in utterly incomprehensible behaviors—flashes of rage or panic, self-destructive behavior, lies, outbursts. "Thai culture," a lot of men say. "Psychological scars from a life of prostitution," I say.

8. In Thai culture, you are defined by the company you keep. And you, as a foreigner, are deemed lower-value if you are known to hang out with or date or even give your custom to prostitutes. Because foreign men are known for going to Thai prostitutes, you are going to have to answer a question from any Thai non-prostitute (or her parents) you meet: have you ever had a bargirl girlfriend? Do you like bargirls? Do you go to the foreign prostitution bar areas? I think if you say you have never, ever had any attraction to any prostitute in your life, you may be seen as a liar—though if it's true, maybe you should stick to it. A much better answer might be that on your first day in Thailand, you went to check out the prostitution areas, but decided it wasn't for you. If you have a long string of bargirl ex girlfriends or ex wives, or even one, you are considered undateable by a large proportion of Thai women. (Well, even in your country—if a man announces that his previous wife was a prostitute—wouldn't that be a turnoff for many women and their families? Thailand is much more restrictive and rule-bound than the West.)

There's a rather crude saying in Thai: you can drink milk, but don't bring the cow into the kitchen. The meaning is that visiting prostitutes as a customer is alright, but getting into deeper entanglements with a prostitute is a bad idea.

That's definitely a dehumanizing view of prostitutes. But that's Thai culture for you. And I do think that this saying, while it's dehumanizing and sexist, has some truth to it.

I think the reason many men so eagerly get into relationships with prostitutes is that they confuse the prostitute's "game face" or "customer-facing personality" with her real self—and they think that dating or marrying her will be a nonstop repeat of the experience she gives her customers. If the customer keeps paying, maybe that will be true. But otherwise, a prostitute becomes a real person, like anybody else—and in the case of a prostitute, probably not someone you want to date or marry.

The "Magical Powers" Test

Here are common ecstatic reports from some guys who've just met Thai women:

"She just came up to me [on the street / at a bar/ at a club / at the mall] and invited me to her apartment!"

"I just looked at her, and she gave me her phone number!"

"She was sitting next to me on the Skytrain and she just asked me to follow her to her home."

"She messaged me on [app/website] and showed me her body and she's my girlfriend now!"

"She's had sex with only one guy before me, but she had sex with me on our first meeting."

"She likes me because I'm a foreigner. We treat women better than Thai guys do."

And then if you challenge the guy and try to discreetly tell him that his girlfriend is a prostitute, he says, "No, no, she's not a prostitute, she never asked me to pay her for sex!"

Do you know how that sounds to a Thai person? It sounds like this: "No way, dude. She's not a hooker. She doesn't have sex for cash. I paid her with a check."

If you were in your hometown, and an attractive (or even unattractive) woman approached you on the subway and suddenly invited you to come to her home and have sex with her, what would you say? Unless you were a celebrity and she was a groupie, you would assume she's under the influence of something, or she's mentally ill, or there's a scam or robbery awaiting you, or she's a prostitute. You—if you are over the age of twelve, anyway—would not say "wow, a random chick just offered me sex on the subway—that new Old Spice cologne I bought must be working!" Right? So why is it that you think it's any different if this happens in Thailand?

I know why. Thai women have a reputation for being hyper-sexual. For being easy to get to bed. For doing anything to get a foreign cock. Or having sex with a foreigner just to have a bed to sleep in. Yes, yes, I know. If you tell a white American that you met a Thai girl, or you met a girl in Thailand, I know: everyone will assume she's a prostitute. And then they'll throw in a few jokes about "does she have a bigger dick than you?" I know. But guess what. Those stereotypes come only from observing prostitutes. And I would say they're not even true for prostitutes. Even prostitutes aren't madly hypersexual. They're just trying to make money.

Anyway, here's the point: if it seems too good to be true—well, you know the rest. Don't assume it's any different just because you're in Thailand. As much as I've told you that Thailand is different from your home country, in this one regard, Thailand is just like your home country. If a woman acts in a highly unusual way that makes you think maybe you have magical powers in this country, something's wrong. Especially because overall, in general, Thai women are probably less open to sex than women in your country.

But—but—but—here's the good news. If you play your foreigner cards right, you can gain an edge, and maybe do better dating in Thailand than in your home country. But it's going to require careful study and consideration. And you still won't have magical powers.

Imagine you walk into a casino. You've never had much luck with casino games, but in this casino, every game you walk up to, you win the jackpot. Every time. Would you assume that you suddenly became an expert at casino games? Or would you begin to suspect that something is wrong—maybe those chips aren't real or maybe you're going to be mugged or drugged or whatever else? You'd be smart to be wary if the casino suddenly started trying to pay you the jackpot every time, for no reason.

But consider if you haven't had much luck with casino games back in your home country. Then you decide to study up a lot on casino games in your new country. You read and study a lot. And you find out how to get a slight edge. You come to the new country, and you try your luck at casino games, and you're not hitting the jackpot every time. But you're doing well. You're doing markedly better than you did in your old country. You occasionally bust and you occasionally have setbacks and you occasionally lose big. But overall, thanks to your study and preparation, you've got a bit of an edge. And you're not doing too bad.

That's how it's going to feel if you read this book. You're not going to have women chasing you down the street to jump into your bed—because, as we already covered, such women are likely prostitutes. But you are going to do quite well for yourself. And isn't that all that any of us can reasonably expect?

8 Red Flags: Tattoos, Smoking, and English

First-world Western societies despise stereotypes. But Thailand is such a regimented society, as compared to the West, that stereotypes actually work pretty well. Thai people almost universally act in the way they're expected to act. And the following are going to be indicators that she is a hooker—not because Thai prostitutes are made from different carbon than Thai non-prostitutes, but because Thai non-prostitutes know very well not to do any of these things, lest they be branded a prostitute.

1. Tattoos. Any tattoo, anywhere. I know: in your country, a doctor or lawyer or judge or professor can have tattoos. Not so in Thailand. Any woman in Thailand who has a tattoo has some link to the sex industry. Even if it's a small tattoo. Even if the tattoo looks just like the one that your mother or your school teacher back home has. Any Thai woman with a tattoo is or has been some sort of prostitute. That's it. And we Thai people know this rule very, very well.

2. Smoking cigarettes. Most Thai women who smoke cigarettes are prostitutes. The only exception would be young, urban "party girls" or "clubbing girls," the kind with a dozen rich Thai boyfriends—and whom you are unlikely to encounter as a foreigner. So as far as you, a foreigner, are concerned, you can assume that any Thai woman who smokes cigarettes is a prostitute.

3. Better spoken than written English. This is a big one. Most Thai people who have some familiarity with English know only written English, and only in the most stilted, formal way that is taught in Thai schools. If a Thai woman speaks English well but can't write English well, she most likely has some experience in foreigner-oriented prostitution. There is some off chance that

she simply hangs around with foreigners a lot—but again, there's all kinds of shades of what "hanging around with foreigners" means, and it's often some sort of prostitution. Ask a Thai woman you met who seems to speak good conversational English to write something for you in English. If she can't, she learned her English most likely in prostitution.

4. Familiarity with sexual terms in spoken English. If a Thai woman is conversant with terms like "blowjob," "dick," "tits," "fuck," "cum," and so on—terms she could not have learned in a Thai school, and could not have learned in American movies (unless they were hardcore porn movies)—she learned in prostitution.

5. Any contact with any aspect of the prostitution industry, such as working as a waitress or cashier in a prostitution venue, hanging out in prostitution areas, or having friends who are prostitutes. I know: the Thai woman you just met swears that she's not a prostitute on Soi Cowboy, only a dancer or a waitress or a cashier. Trust me: she is or was a prostitute. There's a well-known avoidance method of all prostitutes seen in a prostitution venue, when there's some chance of a boyfriend appearing, claiming to be only a waitress or only a cashier or only a dancer or whatever. And because of how regimented Thai society is, no non-prostitute ever, ever would work in a prostitution venue or be seen hanging out in a prostitution venue or befriend a prostitute. Yes, if a Thai woman has friends who are prostitutes, you can be sure she is or was a prostitute. Non-prostitute Thais would never, ever want to befriend prostitutes. That's just how Thai society works. Don't be angry at me, because I didn't invent Thai culture; I'm only telling you about it.

6. Familiarity with Western Union. This is a funny one. But Western Union is the official financial institution of Thai

prostitutes, as they often receive money transfers from abroad. Thai people who aren't prostitutes usually have never even heard of Western Union. You can innocently ask your new Thai acquaintance whether she knows where the nearest Western Union is or whether she knows how to receive money through Western Union. If she's an expert, then she has a connection to prostitution. A close second indicator is familiarity with foreign currency exchange rates, although that could be someone who works in tourism or in an export business.

7. Plastic surgery, especially breast implants, on a woman of modest means. There are two kinds of women in Thailand who get breast implants: rich women and prostitutes. If your Thai ladyfriend is not rich and has breast implants, she got them for her work in prostitution. There's no exception. Why? People who aren't rich in Thailand cannot possibly afford breast implants unless those breast implants are a moneymaking tool (actually though, Thai prostitutes' breast implants are often paid for by their pimps). I know: back in your home country, your grandma and your professor and your accountant got breast implants. I know. But that's in your country, not in Thailand. Breast implants cost about six months' middle-class Thai wages. That would be like costing $25,000 in America. Would a poor American (who most likely had trouble paying the rent) spend $25,000 cash on breast implants just because? Likely not.

8. Online late at night on weeknights, especially around 2-5 A.M. Most people have daytime jobs. Meanwhile, prostitution venues generally close at 2 A.M. Prostitutes often unwind after their workday by going on dating websites. Non-prostitutes usually go on dating websites in the evening, after work, before sleep, say around 8 P.M.. Meanwhile, for prostitutes, that is prime working time, and you will rarely see a prostitute online at that

time (unless she's out of work).

Hi-So vs. Lo-So: Thailand's Class System

Thailand is a structured, regimented society. Every person has his place. And Thai people can be generally divided by two categories: geography and wealth. The two are somewhat related, but not entirely so.

For geography, in Thailand there's a huge divide between urban and rural. In fact, most Thai political conflicts come down to urban vs rural. Urban people are mostly but not entirely from Bangkok.

Rural people are mostly but not entirely from Issan, the poor rice-farming region in Thailand's northeast. (Almost all foreign-oriented prostitutes in Thailand, and most of the people in low-level occupations in Bangkok, are from Issan.) In the Thai mindset, Issan people are equivalent to low, uneducated classes. Of course this isn't always true, and there are many rich people from Issan. But the stereotype of an Issan person is a poor farmer's son or daughter who comes to Bangkok to be either a taxi driver (male) or a prostitute (female). In fact, a vast majority of Bangkok taxi drivers and foreigner-oriented prostitutes are from Issan. I would almost say 100%, but of course that's not true, but I can say almost 100%. (Why only foreigner-oriented prostitutes? Generally Thai men find dark-skinned Issan women unattractive, so they are more drawn to foreign-oriented prostitution.)

The upper class (in Thai slang, "hi so," high society):
Live in Bangkok. Have wealth in real estate and businesses. Send children to private schools or to elite public schools (that require connections to get into). Send children to study abroad, usually in Europe or the US, or sometimes to study at elite Thai universities (Chulalongkorn, Mahidol, Thammasat, sometimes ABAC). Drive exclusively Mercedes and BMW. Household income above $10,000 per month.

The middle class:
Live in Bangkok or nearby, or sometimes in another city. Have wealth in their primary home, maybe in pension investments or a share

of a small business. Can't afford to send children to study abroad, but aspire to send children to elite Thai universities. Drive Toyotas or Nissans or pickup trucks. Household income $1,000-$10,000 per month.

The underclass (in Thai slang, "lo so," low society):

All Thai prostitutes are from this realm. Come from a rural area, but perhaps work in Bangkok. Have wealth in gold and mobile electronics, often worn on the person. Aspire to have children finish high school and attend a low-end Bangkok university such as Ramkamkhaeng or Rajapat. Unlikely to own a car, unless used in farming. Household income under $1,000 a month.

A very useful way to categorize the women you might meet is also by the university they've attended. Here's a basic, very quick rundown that I'm giving you not because you'll be enrolling in a university in Bangkok, but because I want you to have a quick method of judging Thai women you might meet.

Chulalongkorn, also known as **Chula**. This is unequivocally "the best university in Thailand." You have to either have good test scores or great connections to get in here. Some not-rich people do get to go here, and their whole family's social status instantly rises. A "Chula girl" is the most esteemed category of Thai woman to date. A stereotyped "Chula girl" is white-skinned, wealthy, and very, very beautiful.

Mahidol and **Thammasat**. Two universities that are the perpetual #2 universities of Thailand. Maybe they're like Yale and Stanford if Chulalongkorn is like Harvard? Also pretty high-class. Mahidol is particularly known for an excellent medical school. Thammasat is known for rebellious hippie culture, protests and politics, and for an excellent law school.

Kasetsart. Originally an agricultural university ("kaset" means "farm"). Now the #3 or #4 university in Bangkok. Let's say it's the low end of the high end.

ABAC or **Assumption**. Sort of a rich kids' school. Expensive tuition, and instruction all in English. Expect English fluency. Low academic standards, but high standards for English, and high tuition fees.

Silpakorn University. An arts university. Like all arts universities, a hangout for a lot of idle rich kids. Strong associations with the old Thai aristocracy and the idea of being so rich that you can focus your life on art. (By the way, the jazz club I recommend later, Jazz Happens, is closely associated with Silpakorn university.)

Ramkhamhaeng. Derisively called the bargirls' university, because many bargirls formally enroll at Ramkhamhaeng just to be able to say they are university students. Free admission, very low fees. Associated with the rural underclass.

Rajapat. A vocational university strongly associated with the Thai underclass. Notorious for violent and sometimes lethal fights among its students.

Don't Be That Guy: Why You Should Never Wai

Somehow foreigners are fascinated with the Thai "wai," the greeting of raising your hands together to your face. It's complicated. It's traditional. It's not universally done even by Thai people. And it's very, very easy to get it wrong. My advice to you: don't do it. Say hello to people. Shake hands if you'd like. If someone wais you, smile and nod, maybe dip your head a bit if you'd like.

Wai-ing in Thailand maybe is a bit like calling your friends "nigga" in inner-city Detroit. You can do it, and you might see it around you, but if you're a foreigner not conversant in the language and culture, please don't attempt it. Unless you don't think there's anything funny (or dangerous) about a Thai person coming to inner-city Detroit and calling everybody "nigga."

You don't need to learn fluent Thai. And you don't need to try to be Thai. You're a foreigner. That's the point. That's your special appeal.

It's useful to know a few words in Thai for practical things like talking to a taxi driver, but really, you should expect to speak English, not Thai, with your Thai girlfriend. And while Thai people appreciate foreigners learning about Thailand and respecting Thailand—mostly complimenting it—it is cringe-worthy to us when a foreigner tries too hard to superficially imitate some superficial aspect of Thai culture, such as wai-ing or participating in Buddhist religious ceremonies.

Be yourself. Be Mister Foreigner Man. Be respectful and understanding of Thai culture, but don't think you can "fit in" by wai-ing or making similar gestures of Thai-ness, because you will look like a Thai person saying "nigga" in inner-city Detroit, or like a white person wearing blackface in modern America.

The Myth of Sexual Freedom

There's a fairytale told by foreigners: "Thailand is a Buddhist country, so unlike the case in Christian countries, Thai people don't have hangups about sex and sexuality, Thai women don't feel ashamed about sex, and Thailand is accepting and tolerant of all kinds of sexual orientations and lifestyles."

This is one of the most ridiculous things I've ever heard. I don't know exactly how this myth started, although I gather it started with foreigners who believe that what prostitutes do for money represents Thai sexual mores.

Here is the truth, from me, a real Thai girl:

OMG Thailand is the most sexually strict and rule-bound and non-tolerant and non-open country you can imagine!

Seriously. In traditional Thai culture, whatever traditional Thai culture is, unmarried women aren't supposed to hold hands with their boyfriends.

And traditionally, Thai women on their wedding night get a verbal "sex lesson" from their mothers—because they're not supposed to know anything about sex before then of course—and one cornerstone of that lesson is always to never let your husband see you naked! Wear some clothes and you can take some of them off when the lights are completely off but the best idea is never take off all your clothes when you're with your husband, not even for sex, not even in the dark.

That's Thai culture. Of course, not everybody follows that, just as not everybody follows strict Muslim culture in Saudi Arabia or strict Mormon culture in Utah. But that's what we're taught. In fact, Thai university entrance exams have an entire section on "sexual morality," with questions about how to avoid having sex and how terrible it is to go on dates and what are the dangers of homosexuality and so on. Imagine if the American SAT had questions like that. Well, the Thai version of the SAT is full of questions like that.

So you might have some interest in this point if you are an anthropologist, but more likely, you are interested in dating Thai women. I don't want you to have unrealistic expectations. And I don't want you to be shocked when a Thai woman tells you that she will be a virgin until marriage. That is not too uncommon. These days, in Bangkok, it's somewhat uncommon for a girl to completely refuse sex before marriage, but it's not all that uncommon.

And I also don't want you to think that Thailand is "tolerant"—of foreigners with Thai women, of people who are in any way unconventional, or of homosexual and transgender people. In fact, it's very much the opposite. Thailand is very, very regimented, strict, and unyielding. Prostitutes, for example, are very much scorned, and prostitution is formally illegal—the only reason that prostitution operates in Thailand is the government is extremely corrupt and is willing to break any laws in exchange for bribes. It's not because of some kind of "Buddhist tolerance" or anything like that.

Ladyboy Radar

In the last section, I dispelled the myth that Thailand is tolerant and accepting of sexual behavior or sexual orientation. Along with that myth, foreigners often have a myth that Thailand is chock full of ladyboys: biological men who outwardly present (and perhaps inwardly feel) that they are women.

Try this joke, from one of my American friends: "When you bring home a Thai girl, make sure to have two condoms—in case she needs one too."

Or: "I saw a hot Thai girl on the Skytrain and kept saying to myself 'please don't get an erection, please don't get an erection'—but she did."

Ha ha.

The Thai term for a ladyboy, or a male-to-female transgender person, is a "katoey" or "khatoey," but the English term "ladyboy" is commonly known and used. The term "transgender" or "transsexual" is unknown.

For whatever reason, in Thai culture, sexual orientation is all tied up with gender. It is rare to see the two separated. So while in the US, a man who has sexual desire for other men will call himself gay, and will consider his gender still fully male, in Thai culture, such a man will call himself a "woman" (because he has a sexual desire for men) and present to the world as a ladyboy. My opinion, having spent time in the US and UK as well as Thailand, is that Thai "ladyboys" are men who'd be gay men if they had grown up in another country. It's just that Thailand presses them into a different gender.

And no. Ladyboys aren't accepted in Thai culture. There are sad stories of ladyboys being physically attacked and beaten, sometimes to death, in public places. The police doesn't care, or laughs, or joins in. In the Thai policeman's mindset, they're just ladyboys—they're not worthy of police protection. Sorry. That's how it goes.

Similarly, it's difficult for a ladyboy (or an openly gay man) to have a job in any job category that's not specifically associated with ladyboys.

Ladyboys are accepted in cosmetics and beauty, fashion (clothing sellers), entertainment—and prostitution. If a transgender person in Thailand wanted to be a lawyer or a soldier or a teacher or a stockbroker, they'd be very, very unlikely to be accepted. (However, there are some exceptions: ladyboys from very rich and powerful families are able to get around these restrictions. As with most things in Thailand, the rich and powerful can get around the rules other people must follow.)

Additionally, Thai boys who show any "feminine" qualities face strong reprimands from their families and teachers. There are specific Buddhist camps and schools set up to "un-ladyboy" or "make manly" young Thai boys who are suspected of having some aspect of transgender or homosexual behavior. No, Thai Buddhism and Thai culture don't accept fluid gender identities.

Usually ladyboys are completely rejected by their families and any friends they had before they came out as transgender. Some women may not mind befriending ladyboys, although it's seen as a bit of a low-class thing. "Manly" Thai men absolutely do not befriend ladyboys, unless to use as a sexual outlet. That rejection by mainstream society is why in Thailand you almost always see ladyboys in groups, seldom alone. It's all they can do to protect themselves.

So, transgender people in Thailand aren't allowed to have "normal" jobs, and they therefore flock to the prostitution business. And most commonly, they flock to the foreigner prostitution business, because foreigners are seen as unable to recognize a ladyboy from a biological woman, and are also seen as more likely to consciously desire an encounter with a ladyboy. For the same reasons, there are many ladyboys on foreigner-oriented Thai dating sites; sometimes they are honest about their gender identity, and sometimes they are not.

Overall, outside of sex tourism venues and dating websites, there aren't that many ladyboys in Thailand. But if you are a single, foreign male in Thailand, then you will attract ladyboys.

I think we should respect ladyboys, just as we should respect all people. But I agree that you shouldn't date someone you don't want to date. If you want to date ladyboys, that is perfectly fine by me, but please be aware that mainstream Thailand will not approve of your relationship, nor of your ladyboy girlfriend. It's up to you how to deal with that. And if you don't want to date ladyboys, it's quite easy usually to identify a ladyboy. Whether or not you're interested in dating ladyboys, here are some easy ways to identify them, offline or online:

1. There is a stereotypical ladyboy "hair flip." Ladyboys are always playing with their hair, flipping it, and especially tugging it down to cover their masculine jawlines.

2. Height. Thai women are seldom taller than about 165 cm, about 5'5". Of course, not every 5'7" woman is a ladyboy, but it's something like a red flag. (To make things more confusing: 170 cm or 5'7" is considered the female height ideal, and many Thai women will lie about their heights, claiming to be 170 cm or so, when in reality they are much shorter. Conversely, ladyboys who are over 170 cm tall will often claim to be 170 cm.)

3. Big hands, big feet—you know the story. Adam's Apple is not a reliable method, as some biological women have Adam's Apples, and many biological men don't have them.

4. Online photos that hide hands and shoulders.

5. In an online photo or an offline social group, if one person in the group is a ladyboy, you can be about 99.9% sure that everyone in the group is a ladyboy. So if you are unsure about a certain woman's ladyboy status, but she hangs out with a ladyboy (in a photo or in person when you meet), you can be pretty sure she is a ladyboy. Mostly only ladyboys hang out with ladyboys. (One exception is that biological women who are prostitutes do sometimes hang out with ladyboy prostitutes—same line of work and same level of rejection by mainstream Thai society.)

6. The Thai female beauty ideal is tall, slim, and white-skinned. If you meet a Thai woman who is tall, slim, and white-skinned, and seems romantically very pushy or desperate, you should suspect she's a ladyboy. Simply put, a biological Thai woman who is tall, slim, and white-skinned is usually overwhelmed with Thai romantic suitors. If she isn't, there's some chance she's a ladyboy.

7 Places Good Girls Actually Go

Now that I've told you about hookers and ladyboys, let's talk about non-hookers and non-ladyboys and how to meet them. Thai women are 50% of the Bangkok population! And most of them aren't hookers or ladyboys! Fish in a barrel, right? No, not really.

Don't do what a lot of guys do. Don't approach strangers and ask for their phone number. It's happened to me on Skytrain (mass transit) in Bangkok. It's happened to my friends. Somehow Western men see the "friendliness" of prostitutes in the prostitution areas of Bangkok and then decide that all Thai women are eager to meet them.

Usually on Skytrain or at a Starbucks or at a shopping mall, a Western man will come up to a Thai woman minding her own business and say something like "Hi, I'm John, and I think you're very pretty, can I have your phone number?" Most Thai women don't speak enough English to even really understand what was said, but they can guess from the tone of the approach. And they will give one of two responses. If they are prostitutes, they will gladly give their contact information, and perhaps ask to immediately join the foreigner at whatever he's doing at that moment. This is not because he has magical powers; this is because the women are prostitutes, and they were likely in that place to hunt for foreigners in the first place. If they are not prostitutes, they will stare blankly, maybe smile uncomfortably, maybe politely say something like they're busy, or maybe pretend not to understand at all, or maybe say they don't have a phone. That's really not the worst part. The worst part is that everyone around you when you attempt this will look at you as if you were the worst sort of sex offender. Actually when Western guys have approached me in this way, I was only slightly annoyed by them bothering me, but I felt really sorry for the nasty stares and sometimes pointing and laughing they got from my Thai compatriots. In fact, if you do this with the wrong kind of Thai people—say, in a rough area at night—you can easily, very easily, be physically attacked or shot.

Approaching strangers is really not done in Thailand. If you were a Thai guy asking me for dating advice, I'd tell you to never, ever approach strangers. But if you're a foreigner, or at least a white foreigner, you get a bit more leeway. And this is what you can do in public—still not a great way to meet women, and I don't really recommend it, but if you're going to do *something* to meet strangers in public, then this is the way I recommend doing it—get some business cards. Either your real business cards, if your job sounds fancy enough, or some fake business cards if you want to be a BS artist.

Make sure the business card has your Thai phone number and your WhatsApp or Line ID. Thai people don't use email unless it's at work. And you can include your Facebook ID, but interacting with you on Facebook would reveal her connection to you to her friends, and reveal her life to you, so you usually won't get her Facebook until later. Also make sure that your business card has some indication of what country you're from (or claim to be from)—preferably the US or UK.

I didn't think up the fake-business-cards idea myself. A friend of mine once was handed a business card that claimed that the guy who handed it to her was the CEO of United Airlines. Conveniently, "the CEO of United Airlines" had printed on his business cards a Gmail email address, a Thai cellphone number, and his Line and WhatsApp IDs. I mean, what airline CEO doesn't put his Line ID on his business card, right?

Another friend of mine got a business card with a CIA logo. It's great how "CIA agents" identify themselves so readily to college girls they want to pick up! (Actually, she didn't even know what "Central Intelligence Agency" means—she thought it was some kind of educational institution—and the reason I found out is that she showed me the card.)

If I don't recommend handing out fake business cards to meet women, what do I recommend?

The absolute best way to meet Thai women is to have Thai friends, male or female, friends who travel in the same circles as the women you want to meet. If your only Thai "friends" are bargirls, you're not going to meet anyone but bargirls. You need to get out of that world.

One of the best shortcuts to this is to befriend and hang out with some Thai guys. Thai guys generally would love to meet and hang out with foreign guys. The problem is they know that almost all foreign guys (well, the heterosexual ones, anyway) are only interested in Thai women for relationships and sex, not in Thai guys for regular guy hanging-out stuff. If you manage to make friends with Thai guys, you will in general first go through a "trial period" where you'll be checked out by the guy and his buddies—and then you will be presented with a nonstop flow of hot, educated, well-off women who are not on any dating sites and have never been to a bar in their lives.

How to make friends with Thai guys? I suggest thinking about what your interests are, and seeking out Thai guys in those communities. I know one guy in the U.S. who loves old sports cars. When he went on an extended vacation to Thailand, he met up with some classic car clubs in Bangkok. The other members of those clubs were almost exclusively middle-aged, upper-income Thai men who were delighted and amazed to have a foreigner in their ranks—and who very quickly began inviting him to coffees and lunches and so on, with the very clear purpose of introducing him to lots of Thai women.

Another idea is to join one of the many social or language-exchange websites popular in Thailand—such as meetup.com , tagged.com, thaifriendly.com , livemocha.com , and thailandfriends.com—and talk with guys who seem like they share your interests and probably circulate with the kinds of women you want to meet and date. Fortunately, while in Western countries, a man contacting another man on a dating website rings all the gay alarm bells (not that there's anything wrong with that!), it's not so in Thailand—although if you want, you can feel free to write in your profile or your introductory message that you're not gay and just want to be friends.

What about picking up in clubs, not the girlie bars but the clubs where Thai people party, such as the ones on Thonglor and Ekkamai and at RCA?

It doesn't work if you are not in a group of Thai people. It just doesn't. If you are alone, or in a group of foreigners, you will be, at best, politely turned down and ignored, or at worst, kicked out of the club, or at very worst, kicked in the shins and then kicked out of the club. But if you are with a group of Thai guys, this is how "pickup" works in a Thai club:

In Thai clubs, people hang out with their groups of friends, around tables. There's no solo-operator kind of thing.

If there's a woman you're interested in talking to, you can't directly approach her. You talk to your crew who's with you, and you tell them you're interested in talking to that girl at that table over there. By the way, you should look worthy of talking to. That means your clothes should impress. In Thailand, of course, "surface appearances" are reality. If you look high-status, you are high-status.

Some guys from your crew go over to that other table, often without you, and toast whoever seems to be in charge at that table, usually the most "alpha" looking man, and make small talk and say hey great time tonight, great club. If that head man is unreceptive and brushes them off, they scurry back to your table, and it's your signal that none of the women in the group are available. If, on the other hand, the leader of that other table returns the toast and the small talk, you will be invited to come mingle with his group. That's your chance to talk with the women in the group and try to show them that you have a lot of status and face and can show them a good time and potentially be a good companion. It's a good time to have business cards prepared, although that may make you look too scripted and too much like a tryhard. It is more natural to have an expensive phone, an expensive watch, and at least presentable clothes.

It's like that song that goes "have your friends talk to my friends." All of Thai society works like this. If you want a job at a Thai company, it's rare to approach the company directly or to look at their public job listings. Mostly you talk to your friends who work there, and they talk to the people they know who have friends in the hiring department, and so on. That's why in Thailand it's so common that your group of high school or college friends—even for college-educated people—becomes your group of coworkers.

That's club meetings, though. And I don't recommend meeting long-term romantic partners in clubs. Yes, in the US, I know, many great long-term couples met in clubs. In Thailand, sure, it happens, but going to clubs is more of a "party girl" thing—a little bit stigmatized—even though in Thailand, you go to a club to hang out with your friends, not primarily to meet new people. And guess what: the best Thai girls, the smartest, nicest, most trustworthy Thai girls don't go to clubs. At all. A good fraction of my Thai female friends are around thirty years old, grew up in and live in Bangkok, are not poor, are not unattractive, and have not been to a nightclub even once in their lives. The rest go to a nightclub maybe once or twice a year. None of my friends are regular clubgoers—of course, that is just my set of friends, who are more on the homebody side of things. But most good Thai girls are homebodies. A good girl who likes to go out and party at clubs is much rarer in Thailand than it is in the West.

Much much much better than nightclubs—where it's loud and dark and you can't really see or hear people anyway—is that once you have some Thai friends, you join them on their excursions or activities. Once you are in a group like that, it becomes much more natural for your group to potentially socialize with another group—perhaps at a restaurant or a coffee shop. Or a club, meaning a group of people who enjoy some activity you enjoy, not a nightclub, which is a group of people doing who-knows-what. Or even what Thai people sometimes call a "country club"—which can sometimes be like a Western country club, but more often is a clubhouse for the residents of a gated community—and if you have Thai friends who live in gated communities, those can be a great place to meet Thai women who speak English and aren't hookers.

Specific offline places in Bangkok to meet good Thai girls

None of these places are popular with foreigners. That's the point. You avoid the golddiggers and the prostitutes, and you avoid the hordes of other foreign men. You are likely to be the only foreign man there, maybe the only foreign man they've seen in a long time. For all these places, it's always better to go with a Thai group, perhaps a group of both guys and girls, or even just guys.

Tarad Rot Fai, "Train Market"

Central Phraram 9 ("Rama 9"), behind shopping mall

Friday, Saturday, Sunday evenings, around 8 PM - midnight

20-30 year old, middle class women, often in all-female groups

There's no train at Train Market. It takes its name from its previous location, which was in a rail yard, but its new location is not near any rail yards. It's a night market with lots of food and nightlife and bars. The original purpose was selling "vintage" goods, but it has grown way beyond its purpose. People are relaxed, snacking and mingling and sometimes sitting at the streetside bars sipping drinks and listening to music performances. You should really, really go with a Thai group, because the people who work here usually don't speak English.

Note: Train Market is a bit out of the city, toward the airport. Taxi fare about 100 baht one way but drivers may ask for more. Taxi drivers generally hate to go here, and may tell you that it's already closed down or it's not good and you shouldn't go there. On the other hand, getting a taxi from here back to central Bangkok is really, really easy. And of course, getting there by MTR is the easiest way of all (the stop is Phraram 9 / Rama 9).

Starbucks Langsuan

Soi Langsuan, big Thai-style house, can't miss it

Any time

University students, relaxing rich girls, some office workers

This may be the nicest Starbucks in Bangkok, and the area around it is a haven of high-class condo buildings, expensive old-money houses, and high-end expat apartments. Rich women flock here. They're not desperate for dates. But if you want to mingle with that crowd, this is the place.

Starbucks All Seasons Place

Thanon Witthayu (Wireless Road), next to Conrad Hotel, near US Embassy

Office lunch time or during office hours

Office workers

All Seasons Place is located in the midst of lots and lots of company offices, in addition to embassies, and therefore is the Bangkok epicenter of cute, single twentysomething-year-old office girls and professionals on any weekday. However, they're usually with their coworkers and sometimes bosses, so they may feel socially obligated to turn down any advances from you; this would be a good place to hand out a business card to a woman you like.

Au Bon Pain Thonglor / J-Avenue

Thonglor Soi 15, J-Avenue shopping center

Weekday evenings, weekend mornings

This Au Bon Pain traditionally has been where Bangkok's upper and middle-upper class has gone for leisurely snacks before nightlife or leisure breakfasts before shopping. Good place to mingle if you aim high. But nowadays it's declining in popularity because there's a big contingent of, yes, foreigner-bargirl couples.

Banrie Coffee

Corner of Sukhumvit and Ekkamai

Open 24 hours. At night, it's a college students' study hangout. On weekend evenings, it's a beer garden outdoors on the ground level.

This is an old-fashioned Thai tea and coffee house that prides itself on its Thainess. It can be a little bit daunting without Thai friends, because the drink menu is only in Thai, and even the prices are only written in traditional Thai numerals. It used to be completely unknown among foreigners, but nowadays they've started doing the beer-garden thing in the evenings, and sometimes you see foreigners there, perhaps brought by their Thai girlfriends.

Fitness First (Gym) at Terminal 21

6th floor, Terminal 21 shopping center, Sukhumvit

Early mornings and late afternoons (before and after work hours)

Here's where cute up-and-coming office girls go to exercise. You can get a day pass. You can go to a spinning or yoga class. The population is about 80% female. But don't assume every woman is single or looking.

Too Fast To Sleep

Phraram 4 (Rama 4) near Silom

Open 24 hours

This big all-night cafe is the best hangout for somewhat upscale Thai university students. If you look too old, you may feel uncomfortable there. As always, it is better to go with Thai friends, and bring a book to read or a laptop or something, so you don't look like a lecher.

Kinokuniya Bookstore

Siam Paragon Mall

Weekday evenings or anytime on weekends

The English-language section of this big bookstore will let you meet two rare categories of Thai women: those who read books, and those who are brave enough to read in English! It's something like Barnes & Noble in the US—you can wander and browse and perhaps make small talk, or just hand someone your card.

Jazz Happens

Pra-Athit Road, near Khao San Road

http://www.facebook.com/jazZhappens/

Weekend evenings

Jazz Happens, a jazz bar, is a hot (like popular) place for Thailand's art and music community. There are no foreigners here, unless they've spilled over from Khao San Road. Most of the patrons are well-off university students, many of them female, most of them studying fine art or music subjects. They speak English. It's a bit crowded and it's not a place to dance or pick up, but if you can strike up conversations about jazz music, or hand out a business card that shows off your artistic or intellectual street cred, Bob's your uncle.

Digital Minefields: Filter Out Foreigner Hunters

If you don't have a group of Thai friends, then you can let a website perform the same role as a group of friends would perform—introducing you to women, promoting your virtues to them, and letting you screen the good from the bad. The disadvantage of this is that only a small fraction of Thai women is on dating websites, and the most desirable women are rarely on them. Still, many, many very good women use websites, and if you don't have a group of Thai friends or don't have time to go out meeting Thai women in Thai social settings, then a website is your best bet.

The other major advantage of a website is volume. Going around cafes and office parties, you can meet a few women every day. On a website, you can meet as many women as you have patience for—easily more than ten a day. The other advantage is that on a website you can more easily ascertain a woman's English level, age, and basic stats. (I remember a white American friend of a friend who asked me to introduce him to an attractive girl he and I saw on the Bangkok Skytrain—I recognized she was wearing a middle-school uniform! Um, no! He thought she was in her twenties.) Of course, there's lying on a website just as anywhere else—but having at least some representation of what a woman says her age, marital status, educational level, and employment are gives you a very good starting point.

Some websites to explore: thaifriendly.com , thaicupid.com , and tagged.com. The usual US-centric dating websites, such as OkCupid and PlentyOfFish, are used in Thailand primarily by "foreigner-hunting" women that I recommend avoiding, so I recommend avoiding those US-centric websites.

Thaifriendly has a facade of "making friends in Thailand"—of course everybody knows that means Thai women meeting foreign men. In comparing Thaifriendly and Thaicupid, I'd say Thaifriendly has a more cosmopolitan, more English-speaking Thai female population, and that also means more "foreigner hunters." Thaicupid is more likely to have women who have never met a foreigner in their lives. Women on Thaifriendly may be more open to casual dating and women on Thaicupid may be more intent on the marriage track—but that is a very casual generalization and of course you can't expect it to always hold true.

On both Thaifriendly and Thaicupid, you should buy a paid membership—this allows you more functionality in contacting women, but, more importantly, it shows women that you are serious, or you have ten dollars to spare, or something like that.

Tagged.com is almost unknown in the US, but it's huge in Thailand. The nice thing about Tagged is it's 100% free. The other nice thing is you can casually chat and look at each other's photos and so on, without so much pressure to meet or get into a relationship. You can pretend to be "just interested in making friends," which provides a good layer of plausible deniability for Thai women who don't want to be seen as playing the field.

Another excellent but often-overlooked option: interpals.net. Here I strongly suggest your profile location to be your home country. Interpals is a site expressly made for meeting foreign people, so people usually search by location, and they always search outside of their own country. That means that if you set your location to be Thailand, you can expect to make friends with people everywhere *but* Thailand. So you should set your location to your home country, then mention in your profile that you are visiting or plan to visit Thailand.

Interpals has its share of foreigner hunters, but also a very high population of quite high-class university girls who want to practice English. Bad news: many of them may have boyfriends or may really only want to practice English. Good news: some of them might be open to dating a foreigner, or might become open to it once they see how handsome and charming you are. (How old is too old to be dating a university girl? If you're in your thirties, it's ok. If you're forty or older, it's a bit weird, but not unheard of.)

Office Girl: Why She Actually Wants You

If you're meeting Thai non-hookers, and are restricting yourself to exclude let's say the very rural and very poor women, then there is one specific type of Thai woman you'll find in great abundance online, and will almost never find by trying to meet strangers offline, and will never meet in bars or clubs:

She is in her mid or late twenties. Maybe she's from Bangkok or maybe she's from another Thai city. Her parents are civil servants or teachers or own a small grocery store or restaurant; they're not poor but not rich. She attended a good university in Bangkok, graduated with decent grades, and got an office job. She grinds away as an accountant or customer sales rep or project manager, eight or ten hours a day, making about $1,000 per month, which is a very good salary in Bangkok, but is still not a lot of money.

She's just broken up with her first or second ever boyfriend. He's a Thai guy, maybe a classmate or a coworker or a family friend. Now she's 25 or 28 and 30 is looming—and a Thai woman really has to marry by 30. It used to be by 25, but now, in the city, it's 30. And she just wants to give a foreign guy a shot. She's sometimes heard foreign guys are great, other times heard that they're terrible—she wants to find out on her own.

She's seen foreign guys in the city, but they were seldom to her liking. They were either elderly English teachers with bargirl wives, or young backpackers who looked shady and unreliable. Her dream foreign guy would be one of those expat executives she's heard of—the ones who have six-figure USD salaries and private drivers and rooftop condos, the ones who look like magazine models. But she doesn't need that expat CEO kind of guy literally. She just wants someone respectable and reliable and predictable, someone who doesn't feel wild and unpredictable—but has a little bit of that exotic foreign flavor, maybe can help her improve her English, maybe can teach her about foreign cultures, maybe even travel internationally sometime.

There's a Thai guy at the office who's after her. Her first boyfriend also wants her back. One of her neighbors is also chasing after her, and showing off his new BMW to try to lure her. Those are all options. But she wants to try a foreign guy just once. And a friend of a friend met a great foreign guy online and married him, and she wonders if she could match that kind of luck. She just doesn't want to meet the kind of foreigner she always hears about, who is drunk, jobless, and promiscuous.

She'll meet you for a first date after work at the MK or Fuji restaurant adjacent to the building where she works. She'll symbolically offer to pay for the meal, or pay her share of the meal, because she's heard that's how it's done in foreigner-land, but she'll love it when you insist on paying anyway. You can let her pay for coffee or dessert later in the evening just to give her some face and show that you don't think of her as destitute.

At your first date, you explain that you enjoy Thailand, that you were intrigued by her profile online, that you want to spend more time with her and get to know each other. You do *not* talk about your dick or ask her if she is good at blowjobs or what sexual positions she's tried. Somehow foreign men get this idea that these are normal conversation topics in Thailand. Maybe they're normal conversation topics with prostitutes, when you're a customer—and most foreign men first experience Thai women as customers of prostitutes. Let me assure you though, even Thai prostitutes don't like talking about this stuff with their real boyfriends. They only talk about it with foreign customers because they know that's what's expected.

Yes, there will be sex: usually after a few weeks of evening meetings, you will invite her to eat a meal at your condo or hotel room, or to listen to your music collection, or to help you practice Thai, or whatever else. She will be shy and will say her body isn't nice and her breasts are too small. She may also say that no one has given her oral pleasure before. She won't yell "fuck me good!" or any of those other bargirl things, because she's not a bargirl. But you'll enjoy the sex. Or you should enjoy the sex.

She won't require marriage or a guarantee of marriage before she has sex with you and introduces you to her parents. That may have been true fifty years ago, but no longer. But she will need to know that there's a good chance of marriage: that you are single, that you are financially self-supporting, that you are someone she wouldn't mind shacking up with for the long term. If those are not fulfilled, she is unlikely to follow you into the bedroom.

On that subject: accepting an invitation to your condo or hotel room is equivalent to accepting an invitation to sex. I know that in America it's normal for your female friend or your date to come over to your home and it's not necessarily an invitation to sex. Thailand is different. So you may shock her if you invite her to your hotel room—even if you didn't mean anything sexual by it—too early in the relationship. Relatedly, Thai people don't visit one another's homes, unless they are very close friends or family; otherwise, they meet in restaurants or coffeeshops or other public places. There are no home dinner parties in Thailand, unless it's either a family gathering or a very Westernized Thai person trying to play up a Western lifestyle.

Profile Fix: Stop Looking Like a Sex Tourist

You don't want to seem desperate. You don't want to seem sexually aggressive or dangerous—that's the negative stereotype she's heard about foreigners. But you do want to seem assertive, confident, and successful enough for her to want to go out of her way—her usual "way" being dating Thai guys—to date you.

1. Your profile picture must show you wearing nice clothes. Your main profile picture must not be inside your home, unless your home looks like a palace. It should be either at your work or office or a place that you can claim is your work or office, or show you doing something like traveling. Travel is associated with prestige and wealth for Thai people. Show yourself in some "exotic" places, especially with iconic stuff like the Eiffel Tower or the Grand Canyon. Do not show yourself with other women, even if they're your friends or relatives. Do not show yourself sad or aggressive or scary or making weird faces or wearing scary makeup.

2. Your profile must clearly show why you're a good guy. Use simple English that a nonnative speaker can understand. Don't use slang or sarcasm. Show that you are a happy, pleasant guy to be around. Never, ever use your profile to complain about Thailand or about your job or about your ex or about anything else. Never, ever.

3. When you message women, say something specific about her profile—something other than their physical appearance. Say that you share a hobby they mention. Say you saw a movie they liked. Say you visited a place they visited. Say you want to learn a sport they play. This shows that you are a listener, you read her profile, you are interested in her and focusing on her, and not

mass-mailing everyone on the site or going only by pictures.

4. Never, ever say anything sexual in your profile or in any initial chat. Never, ever, ever, ever.

5. Move to email or Line or WhatsApp or Skype. If possible, minimize how often you log on to the dating site—to show her that you are focusing on her, and not still playing the field. Keep your messages to her short, frequent, and cheery. Make yourself a bit of happiness in her dreary day.

First Date Blueprint: MK, Fuji, and Who Pays

There's a Thai joke.

Q: When does a foreigner have sex with his Thai girlfriend, in relation to the first date?

A: The night before.

Yes, that's the general Thai impression of foreigners' relationships with Thai women. That they have sex with a bargirl, then decide to start dating her. And it is overwhelmingly true in many cases. But let's talk about the rest of Thai female society.

According to the "Thai experts" I've seen online, a first date with a Thai woman always includes a chaperone brought along by the woman. According to those "Thai experts," every "good Thai girl" brings a chaperone, usually an aunt, to a first date.

That bit of cultural information was true—in the 1950s. I don't know where they're getting this, but it's really not true now, at least not in Bangkok. It was true in Bangkok seventy years ago and even fifty years ago, but not now. And now, it may be true in some very traditional families in some very rural places in Thailand, but it would be considered ridiculous in Bangkok. I've just never heard of it from any of my contemporaries, and I'm a thirty-year-old Bangkokian.

Now, once you are in a relationship with a Thai girl, especially a "good Thai girl," you will be expected to meet her parents, or at least her mother, as a marker of the relationship being serious. I guess this is also true for relationships in the US, but in Thailand, the parental-meeting will come sooner and will be more important than it would be in the US.

As for what happens on the first date: if you and she have already talked, probably online, then it will likely be one-on-one. If you and she don't know anything about each other, then it will be a pre-date, something where you and she can get to know each other in a group setting, and likely, her friends can inspect you. For example, she will invite you to join her and her group of coworkers for lunch—very very common. And yes, you will be inspected and dissected and discussed. That's the point.

But if you and she have already talked, whether online or in some offline setting, then you can be pretty sure the date is going to be one-on-one. In fact, if she brings a friend along (unannounced), you can take it as a sign that she and her friend are treating you as a free meal ticket, and she is more interested in a free meal and time chatting with her friend than in meeting you. I would hope that you have performed enough due diligence on her before that first meeting to establish that she's interested in you, and not in a free meal—but in case you haven't, then the friend coming along for the meal, and the two of them having a strong idea about where they want to meet (interpretation: they feel like going to that restaurant but what someone else to pay), is going to be your sign that she's more interested in free food than in you, and that there's likely going to be another foreigner lined up, perhaps by the friend, to provide her and her friend a free meal the next day.

The most popular Thai first date restaurant, ever, ever, ever: MK. I don't know why, but first dates are generally at MK. It's a Thai hotpot restaurant. You sit in front of a pot of boiling water and order meat and vegetables and whatever else to throw into the water to make a stew. It's popular as a first date because it gives you not only a meal, but also an activity of cooking that stew thing together, instead of just staring at each other over plates of food. There's also some collaboration involved in choosing the things to put in the soup and discussing food tastes and all that.

"Where's MK?" Everywhere in Thailand. In every shopping center, every grocery store, everywhere. There's also MK Gold, which is a slightly more expensive and upscale MK. Anyway, don't make a rookie mistake and ask "what's MK?" when your Thai date asks to meet at MK.

The second date is going to be at Fuji. Fuji is a Thai-style chain "Japanese" (wink wink) restaurant, meant for office lunches, family weekend outings—and second dates for middle-class Thais. Trust me on this one. It's going to be Fuji. Fuji is also in every mall and office building, although perhaps in slightly lower numbers than MK. Fuji is a little bit more up-midscale, while MK is mid-midscale.

Subsequent dates may involve movies, a shopping mall, bowling (yes, fashionable in Thailand), maybe a concert or another public event.

At some point, you may want to offer to take her to an expensive rooftop bar/restaurant in Bangkok. There are tons of them, so you may want to ask her which one she wants. These places are way too expensive, maybe $200 USD for two people to have a small meal and drinks—but it shows her that you're capable of providing her an improved lifestyle.

I'll tell you what some sleazy foreign men do as a date idea. I don't advocate it, because it's deceptive and plays on women's hopes, but I'll tell you anyway: go to a sales office for a condo development, and to an expensive furniture store, both times pretending that you're considering moving to Thailand and buying this expensive condo and this expensive furniture, of course with your new girlfriend/wife. I've heard from several friends who have dated foreigners that this is a common tactic, and yes, they did fall for it—and the men later disappeared, without any intention of buying that condo or furniture. Well, I don't condone this "date idea," but it's out there, and if all you care about is getting sex, it will work, but of course it's no way to build a long-term relationship.

Why Rich Girls Cost Less Than Poor Girls

If any Thai woman ever tells you that money doesn't matter in her relationship with you—whether she is rich or poor or in between—she is either delusional or trying to delude you. Money always matters. But, depending on her social position in Thailand—yes, you already know that social position is what matters in Thailand—money is going to matter in different amounts, and in different ways.

Hear me out, because it took me a long time to conceptualize this difference in my head and write it out. I knew it intuitively, but you know the saying: you don't really know something until you write it out (especially in a foreign language!) and have to explain it to someone.

So, after a good long while thinking it out, this is the rule I've come up with: **The higher on the socioeconomic ladder a Thai woman is, the more money you will be required to *have*, but the less money you will be required to *spend*.**

If you date a very poor woman, she will consider you as having enough money even if you're poor back in your own country. But you're going to have to give her a lot of that money, or use it on her.

If you date a very rich woman, she is going to be very picky about your financial status. Of course, not all rich Thai women are the same, but roughly speaking, it's going to be difficult to date her if you don't have about the same level of financial success as her family—or if you can at least fake having it! The good news is that she probably won't be asking you for any of this money. It is very unlikely that you'll be required to spend money on her, other than perhaps something to show off and demonstrate to her, her family, and people whom they want to impress that you have a lot of money.

In the case of dating a rich woman, there are stories about rich parents requiring the husband to present a "sinsod"—a dowry payment—at the wedding ceremony, just to impress everyone with how rich he is, and then he parents return the money to the husband after the ceremony, because they don't need his money, but they want to gain face from his presentation of the money.

That touches on the touchy subject of sinsod, dowry or "bride money." A husband is expected to present the wife's family with some amount of money at the wedding. A fairly standard sum for an upper-middle-class Thai family would be something like two million baht, about $60,000 USD. Yes, it's a lot of money. It basically compensates the woman's family for their daughter's loss of value on the marriage market. Once she's been married (and presumably had sex to consummate it!) she's almost worthless on the marriage market, so you're paying something like a depreciation payment. Two million baht is fairly standard, but five or ten million baht (a few hundred thousand USD) is not unheard of.

Sinsod may not be required if the woman is considered valueless in the first place—old, ugly, previously married. Some extremely understanding and non-traditional parents may not require sinsod, especially if they are not poor. What is most commonly done among upper-crust families who don't want to burden the couple with a sinsod requirement but still want to save face is something what I described above: a sinsod is paid publicly by the groom to the bride's family, but after the wedding, the family quietly returns the money to the groom, or perhaps uses the money to buy a house or a car for the newlyweds.

If you have realistic plans of marrying a Thai woman, you may want to discuss sinsod with her at some point. I think a common refrain you may hear from the woman would be "I don't believe in sinsod, but my parents absolutely require it." It may, indeed, be a deal-killer, especially if her parents won't budge, and if you are morally against "paying for a bride," as many foreign men are. There's no way out, other than perhaps discussing some idea for everyone to save face (perhaps you buying a house in Thailand—which has to be held in your Thai wife's name by Thai law—instead of sinsod?). Otherwise, the only advice I can give you is to discuss the topic early, in case it comes up unexpectedly later in your relationship and ruins an otherwise perfect relationship—which certainly does happen.

Racism and Dating in Thailand

In general, Thai people equate "foreigners" with white people of European descent, from first-world, English-speaking countries. In the Thai mindset—and I'm talking about college-educated, white-collar Thai people, not just bargirls—all foreigners:

Are white

Are from this collection of foreign countries: US, UK, Australia, Canada, France, Germany, Switzerland. That is an exhaustive list of all foreign countries for the average Thai person. I'm sorry, but it's true. By the way, English is the language exclusively spoken by all people in those countries. (And they know Germany and Switzerland because the Royal Family spends a lot of time there.)

Speak English as a native language

Come to Thailand to escape the very cold weather in their native country

Are rich if living outside Thailand, or poor if living in Thailand

If you don't appear to be of European descent, it is going to be very, very difficult for you to get any attention from a Thai woman, with one exception: if you are Korean or Japanese (by nationality or ethnicity), or if you can claim to be Korean or Japanese, you get a free pass, because Korean and Japanese pop culture is popular in Thailand and Korean and Japanese men are seen as cool and desirable.

If you are of African descent (for example, an African American from the US), you are going to have a really, really tough time. Dark skin is seen as a defect, and you will be thought of as something like a violent thug from some kind of American crime movie. I don't know what to tell you, other than not to expect too much, because Thai people are really, extremely racist. They practice the same within Thailand—light-skinned Thai people usually call dark-skinned Thai people monkeys—so it shouldn't be surprising that they act the same toward foreigners. Again. Please don't hate me for telling you the truth. I have nothing against people of any race. But I am not an average Thai person. Perhaps the best advice I can give you is to seek out Thai women who have had experience living abroad, perhaps in the US, and have been around black people and don't see them as dangerous or subhuman.

If you are of South Asian (Indian) descent, you'll be perhaps even worse off than being of African descent. Indians—called "khaek" in rude Thai slang—are universally despised by average Thai people. And, in the Thai mindset, having any physical resemblance to "khaek" (Indians) makes you pure khaek.

In the US I met one American guy whose ethnic ancestry is from India. His grandparents and parents came to the US from India in the 1960s, and he was born in the US and has considered himself fully American all his life.

Well, guess what. When he came to Thailand and tried to meet Thai women: it was really, really, *really* difficult. His initial method was to meet women online and talk honestly about himself—he was born in Boston, he grew up in Los Angeles, he had X job and Y hobbies and so on—without showing a photo. Unfortunately, the first woman he met, at Central World mall, upon seeing him in person, at first had a look of wide-eyed disbelief, then said she had to go to an urgent work meeting, and he never heard from her again. His other experiences trying to date in Thailand were similar. He did have some limited success meeting highly educated Thai women who didn't share the average Thai's racist beliefs, and didn't share the idea that only white people can be Americans—but it was a very, very limited sort of success.

You can generally assume that if you are not white, you will be categorized by Thai people based on your ancestors' country. It doesn't matter if you were born in the US and have never visited China in your life—if your ancestors were Chinese, then you will be thought of and described as the "Chinese" guy she met, and rank a few rungs below the nice "American" (white) guys.

Speaking of Chinese: for some reason, maybe justified or maybe not, Singaporean men have an extremely negative reputation among Thai women. Thai women believe that Singaporean men are all untrustworthy sex tourists. While Singapore itself holds an esteemed position in Thai people's minds, men from Singapore are derided and distrusted. Maybe it's because Singapore is such a close hop from Bangkok tha Singaporean men really do hop over for quick flings. I don't know. But if you're a Singaporean man and want a serious relationship with a Thai woman, it's going to be a severe uphill battle, because there's a strong presumption that you're a liar and a player.

Hong Kong and Taiwanese and Chinese men: no strong reputation that I know of. I think they're just lumped in as "China" ("jin" in Thai), and may benefit from the Thai belief that "Chinese" is a superior race—see the chapter about that in this book—but still lie several rungs lower than white people in Thai women's racial hierarchy.

Dating Thailand's Hidden Aristocracy

Immigrants from China crowded into Thailand in the early and mid twentieth century, and some of those immigrants' descendants joined the ruling classes of Thailand. The whole story of how the Chinese immigrants brought themselves under the King's protection is too long to repeat here, and not very relevant. But this is enough to know: in Thailand, being Chinese (by ethnic heritage) is a point of pride and prestige. Many women you meet in Thailand will point out to you that they're Chinese or part Chinese—sometimes this is true and sometimes it isn't. In your country nobody would actually make up a lie about being Chinese, nor think of being Chinese as their main positive personal trait—but in Thailand, "I'm Chinese" is something like "I'm high-class." (And the Thai pronunciation usually sounds something like "I'm shyness.")

Most of the richest people in Thailand certainly are of Chinese heritage. The Chinese in Thailand own most of the big businesses. And if you look at faculty rosters at major Thai universities or executive rosters at prestigious Thai companies or staff listings at Thai hospitals, you will see a lot of people of Chinese origin. Roughly 10% of the people in Thailand are of some Chinese origin. That goes up to about 20% in Bangkok. But it's not uncommon for any grouping of highly educated or successful Thais to be 100% consisting of those of Chinese origin.

What I will call the "true" Chinese will be those who speak Chinese (usually Teochew, sometimes Hakka or Cantonese) at home, call their mother "ma" and not "me," avoid eating beef, and have a surname longer than four syllables. That last part sounds ridiculous, but it's generally true. People of Chinese origin in Thailand generally have surnames longer than three syllables. Why? The Thai government required Chinese immigrants to find Chinese surnames, and they had to be surnames that no one else in Thailand had, not even one other person. All the short and simple surnames were taken. The Chinese immigrants made new surnames, generally based either on their original Chinese names (for example, Thaksin Shinawatra—his grandfather's original Chinese surname was Shin), or based on some religious or otherwise fortuitous meaning.

Others are those I will call "wink wink nudge nudge" Chinese. Many of the lighter-skinned Thais from the north of Thailand will claim to be Chinese. And people who once heard from a relative that they had a great-great-grandfather who was Chinese will call themselves "Chinese" or sometimes "half Chinese." Does it matter? Not really.

But if you're going to aim for dating the upper echelons of Thai society, you will definitely encounter women from the Chinese ethnic group. There are a few important characteristics to remember about them.

First, aside from sneaking out to party when they can in their college days, Chinese girls are strongly discouraged to go outside the home, unless it's for some very specific and productive purpose, such as going to school, going to work, or conducting family business. Otherwise, they're expected to stay home. There's no "hanging out" allowed. What does that mean for you? It means that you will not find these girls in bars, or even in malls or coffee shops. They are at home. And the only way you can meet them is through their existing social contacts, or online.

Next, generally their parents' (not necessarily the daughters') preference for whom their daughter should date or marry goes like this: 1. Thailand Chinese guy, 2. White guy, 3. non-Thai Asian guy, 4. non-Chinese Thai guy. Put directly: Thai Chinese girls' parents really, really don't want them to bring home Thai Thai (non-Chinese) guys. It is a very strong and very broad prohibition. Is it racist? Of course it's racist! Thailand is racist! But what does it mean for you? It means that you have some leg up at least against the non-Chinese local Thai guys, even if they're rich. For whatever reason, Thai Chinese girls' parents will often prefer a poor and uneducated white guy over a rich and educated Thai Thai guy—and I have seen this myself, when a beautiful and well-educated Thai Chinese friend's father was overjoyed when she dumped her rich and handsome Thai Thai lawyer boyfriend (and true to the parents' stereotypes, he was kind of a player) for a bald, poor white guy who had barely finished high school back in his native Australia.

A lot of Thai girls will claim to be Chinese or Thai Chinese or half Chinese. It's a bragging point. If she is genuinely Chinese, she will be from Bangkok, she will live with her parents, she will be quite well-off, and her movements will be highly restricted. Perhaps the litmus test for "genuinely Chinese" is if she can speak Teochew (the Chinese dialect almost universally spoken by Thai Chinese people). If she can speak more than a few words, then yup, she's Chinese. If not, she's not. (Or if she can only speak Mandarin, she learned it in school or for the tourist industry. Thai Chinese people never speak Mandarin at home.)

Shorts, Sandals, and the Back Strap Rule

One of the myths passed around about polite Thai society—outside of Thailand—is that you absolutely can't wear shorts anywhere but the beach. And that is absolutely false. Go to any fashionable Bangkok place during the day and a lot of fashionable Bangkok residents will be wearing shorts. There's nothing wrong with wearing shorts to a mall, an outdoor market, a casual restaurant, or even a casual date.

I think the myth started fifty years ago, when tourists first started pouring in to Bangkok, and when it was indeed rude to wear shorts in Thailand anywhere but the beach. But guess what: Thailand doesn't stay the same over forty years. It's not Miss Pac-Man days anymore. It's now perfectly acceptable to wear shorts around Bangkok. Speedos or torn jean shorts, maybe not. We don't need to see hairy butt-cheek peeking out from your Daisy Dukes. But normal walking shorts, board shorts, golf shorts, whatever, are all fine.

The only places you can't wear shorts: the Grand Palace (Wat Pra Keaw) and other temples, government buildings and offices (you will be denied entry to a government office if wearing shorts), funeral ceremonies, and other than that, you can use a rule of thumb of "can you wear shorts there in New York City?"—Starbucks, yes, but formal dinner, fancy evening restaurant, fashionable nightclub, no. (Dive bar, yes. See, just like New York City.)

Now, sandals. Not Sandals™, the all-inclusive resort for aspirational middle-class Texans (I told you I work in commercial real estate, right?). Sandals in Thailand fall into two very distinct and very arbitrary categories.

If you were going to categorize Thai ladyboys, one good taxonomy might be: *does she have a cock*? Well, if you are going to categorize sandals in Thai culture, the correct way is: do they have back straps? If they have back straps, they are "polite sandals," and generally ok to wear. If they don't have back straps, they are "impolite sandals," and not ok to wear other than to the beach or to 7-11.

So get your fisherman sandals going. Get your Tevas going. Birkenstocks, only if they're the kind with back straps. Polite sandals. Or you can just be safe and wear some nice clean athletic-type shoes; it would be perfectly polite to wear not-bright-colored running shoes to pretty much any event or social situation in Thailand.

One Joke Can Put You in Prison

You may have heard that Thai people love their King. You most likely have no idea how much. Also, you may have no idea how extremely easy it is to land in a Thai prison for many years for making the most innocuous comment about the monarchy.

I can't even repeat the comments that have landed Thai and foreign people in prison, because repeating them would itself be a crime. But basically, saying anything other than "the monarchy is perfect" is absolutely illegal, and frowned upon. And this is a big deal, not a joke. People go to prison for offhanded, casual remarks. And foreigners also lose their relationships with their Thai friends or girlfriends over seemingly innocuous remarks about the Thai monarchy.

It's better not to bring up the monarchy in conversation. If a Thai person brings up the monarchy, you should say very, very little, other than expressing admiration and respect for the monarchy. I'm serious about this. It's perhaps the most serious thing in Thailand. Don't mess up.

Sinsod, Face, and the Final Inspection

At some point, especially if her parents live in Bangkok, you'll be meeting her parents. It of course depends on how open her parents are to you, and how close your girlfriend is to them. But "I don't care about my parents" is extremely rare, pretty much unheard of, among Thai women. Whether or not she brings you to meet her parents, she still cares very much about what her parents think of you, and by extension, of her.

Meeting her parents is pretty similar to meeting your girlfriend's parents in any other country. You have to be nicely dressed and make polite conversation and talk about your education or your future or something like that. More so in Thailand than anywhere else, you should flash an expensive watch or phone or car or something—rather than being seen gauche, it's seen as a show of your respectability.

One other difference, or at least different in matters of degree, is that in Thailand, you should make an effort to "give face" to the woman's parents. This is done much more consciously in Thailand than in the West. Compliment them, repeatedly and effusively, on the choice of restaurant or the food. Compliment them about their daughter's education and success and good English (don't compliment them about her nice ass, please).

You may want to learn a few phrases of Thai if her parents don't speak English. You don't need to be fluent or anything. But speaking a few words of Thai demonstrates your commitment to Thailand and to their daughter.

Who pays for the meal? Difficult to say. If her father is present, and it's a big family dinner, it's likely that her father would pay. If only her mother is present, you may be expected to pay. I would say that if her father is present, you should not make a motion to pay, as that would be challenging the father's face and authority. If her father is not present, you should at least offer to pay, and be prepared to perhaps have her mother accept the offer.

Don't ever make sexual jokes or anything risque. Don't use sarcasm; Thai people aren't good at understanding it, and you may get in a lot of trouble. Mostly stay quiet, offer compliments, and say something good about yourself, proving what a stable, educated, successful man you are. But that's the same in every country, isn't it?

Conclusion

Thailand is a great place. And as biased as I may be on the topic, I think we Thai girls are pretty great people! With the advice in this book, you can experience the good Thai girls, the ones who don't hang out at prostitution venues, the ones who are off-limits to foreigners who try to date prostitutes or approach strangers on the street.

Please use a good dose of your own common sense together with this book. I can't claim to know everything about every Thai woman ever, but fortunately, Thai women are pretty uniform and pretty predictable, so I think I can reliably say a lot—and I've told you a lot in this book.

Use your own common sense, follow your mind and your heart, and I wish you happiness and love in your own Thai Romance.

-Linda